The Weybridge Sailing Club Monologues

To Charmaine, with all good wishes, Tim (the Cook)

Volume II

Written and illustrated

by

T. J. Carter

T. J. Carter, W.S.C.
18 - 5 - 2020

© 2019 Tim Carter. All rights reserved.
ISBN 978-0-244-84075-4

This book is dedicated to

Neil and Sue Davey W.S.C.

and

all those who love the River Thames.

HKP

Hamley King Publishing
London

CONTENTS

The Parson of Pangbourne's Pike..................……..……7

Old Father's Source……………………...……………….27

The Dames of Wallingford ……………………...……49

The Blue Dahlia………...……………………………..71

The Goblets and the Gondolier…………...………...94

The Last Monologue of Weybridge……………........117

Performance Notes………………………….……..... 145

The Topography of the Monologues...…………..….152

Acknowledgements...……………………….....…….155

The Parson of Pangbourne's Pike

I.

I had a career as a naval lawyer,
But I dropped a couple of clangers,
So I retired to the village of Whitchurch
On the banks of the Thames near "Pangers".

II.

To be honest, I was never much of a sailor –
I chunder at the slightest of swells—
But I became Commodore of Pangbourne Sailing Club,
Assisted by brandy and *Quells*.

III.

We used to store our boats on the island
'Tween the weir and the millstream cut,
And, in the field opposite the Rectory,
We had our little Boat Club Hut.

IV.

Oh, it wasn't much of a clubhouse,
But it satisfied our nautical needs
And, when they asked the old Rector who owned the land,
He said, "I think it belongs … to the grebes!"

V.

The Rector of Whitchurch was a kindly old chap,
Disinclined to give moral strictures,
He preferred to go fishing with his three-legged dog,
For he'd grown tired of reading the scriptures.
(Indeed, he'd read the Old Testament so many times,
He felt a growing sympathy for the Philistines!)

VI.

Each day the Rector took to his punt,
After Matins and a hard-boiled egg,
Hoping to catch the enormous pike
That had scoffed his Jack Russell's back leg.

VII.

I was with the Rector one morning
When another puntsman drew up for a chat:
It was the Parson of Pangbourne, Reverend Finch,
Wearing his tweed fishing hat.

"You'll never catch a pike on paste!"

VIII.

"Still not caught that pike, Rector?"
Boomed the Parson, "Look at the hours you waste!
Why don't you try a live bait?
You'll never catch a pike on paste!"

IX.

"I've hooked that pike myself you know,
On an almighty salmon fly.
That's why he sulks in your millpool.
That's how he lost his right eye!"

X.

"To business… and I bring grave news from the Archdeacon:
His godson… is *sent down* in disgrace!
I speak, of course, of Bunny Stoat the Oxford Stroke,
Who tried to fix the Boat Race."

XI.

"Bunny's father's on his death bed
And, weighed down with foolish pride,
He says he will *cut off* his son,
Unless he weds a loaded bride."

XII.

"So Lady Stoat has made a match
With Lady Breedon's girl Susannah,
Who'll bring plenty of money to Bunny,
As heiress to Pangbourne Manor."

XIII.

"Susie Breedon is a sporty girl
And, in truth, an absolute menace!
She's completely nuts about Gilly Gem,
Whose father invented lawn tennis!"

XIV.

"She says she will only marry Bunny,
And for yonder sailors it's bad news,
If she and Gilly get a tennis lawn
…with stunning river views."

XV.

"Bunny suggests the Sailing Club field,
Since his rowers could do with a mooring.
And, when records are perused, the field they use
Belongs to the Stoats of Goring."

XVI.

"So don't just sit there Rector,
Like Nero playing his fiddle.
Go and tell your Sailing Club friends—
This is the *end* of their riverside idyll!"

XVII.

At noon the Rector conveyed the news,
To assembled Boat Club buffers,
That, with the Archdeacon's blessing,
Their Sailing Club was scuppered!

XVIII.

He said: "Dear friends I'm very sorry, and
I just don't understand,
For my verger once read in the ledger
That this land is *grebe* land!"

XIX.

Then upstream from Pangbourne Meadow
Came the most unlikely pairing of craft—
A fully-manned Oxford rowing eight,
Towing a dainty skiff to its aft.

XX.

Two chunky girls in tennis attire
Reclined astern in the following boat.
Playing gooseberry between 'em, with a rose in his teeth,
Sat the infamous Lord Bunny Stoat!

Playing gooseberry between 'em with a rose in his teeth.

XXI.

"Those dreadful sailors are still in our field,
Gilly!" the chunkier of the two girls shouted.
"I want my tennis lawn and I want it now!
Bunny, do something about it!"

XXII.

Stoat pushed the Rector as he leapt ashore, saying,
"Out of my way – Reverend Codger!"
Then, attaching a line to the Clubhouse piles,
He called: "Full steam ahead please, Roger!"

XXIII.

Roger Smoothly was rowing at Stroke,
That philanderer so aptly named.
His eight tore our Clubhouse from the bank—
At such speed that it aquaplaned!

XXIV.

The old Clubhouse started to list
At the point where the river bends,
And, having passed under the Toll Bridge,
It *sank* to the bottom of the Thames!

XXV.

The rowers bundled us in our dinghies,
With our rigging and our sailing books,
"Shove off you plebs and don't come back!"
Said Stoat, "To put it bluntly, sling your hooks!"

XXVI.

How could the Rector comfort us
When all that we loved had gone?
He just led us back to Pangbourne
And bought us a pint in *The Swan*.

XXVII.

An army of workmen came to the field,
With scythes and mowers the long grass was shorn,
Then, clad in slippers, with paint pots and clippers,
They created a riverside tennis lawn.

XXVIII.

They put up *Pimm's* tents, with bunting and hides for duck hunting
And for the betrothal, a marvellous marquee,
They built pontoons for rowers and sheds for the mowers
And, strictly for ladies…..a W.C.

XXIX.

Susannah and Gilly loved their lawn,
But Bunny seemed unable to please 'em,
They used to play with *Roger* all day
In what you might call a "mixed threesome".

XXX.

It was the evening before the Betrothal
And I was trudging back from *The Swan*,
When I spied a couple of scullers
In the light of the sinking sun.

XXXI.

They were resting 'neath the Toll Bridge,
For they must have rowed several miles
And I heard the voice of Bunny Stoat
Echoing up from the piles.

XXXII.

"My father's gone and snuffed it
And mother sends this warning:
I must get married quick
Before they find him in the morning."

XXXIII.

"If I can argue that I wed
When Dad's not dead but ill,
His solicitor in Reading
Can't cut me from the will."

XXXIV.

"Invite Susannah to *The George Hotel*
Roger, and when I turn up later,
I'll say, 'You'd better marry me quick
Or I'll go to the local paper'."

XXXV.

"We'll get that Rector to marry us —
I'm sure he'll do as we like.
We'll threaten to take his three-legged dog
And throw it to the Pangbourne Pike!"

XXXVI.

"I must stay up!" I told myself,
"So I can see what happens.
I'll watch the Toll Bridge from my lawn
And be at Church for Matins."

XXXVII.

First…
As I watched, the verger entered the toll booth
And soon I heard him snore.
He always slept there when he was drunk
And his wife had locked the door.

XXXVIII.

Then, along came the Rector's dog,
Who sat beside the booth.
He'd come to collect his master's mail
And lay down for a snooze.

XXXIX.

Then, along came Bunny Stoat,
Wearing a bridegroom's kilt and sporran.
He seized and sacked the Rector's dog
As if ferreting at a warren.

XL.

Roger came to the booth when Bunny left
And took two girls inside.
One of 'em emerged as a bridesmaid,
Another was dressed as bride.

XLI.

At first light, I ran to St. Mary's,
But they were singing the final psalms —
For Bunny Stoat was *already* married
And his bride seemed completely "Brahmsed"!

XLII

"Give me a certificate!" cried Stoat.
Said the Rector, "I refuse!
For your best man's got a shotgun
And your bride doth reek of booze!"

XLIII.

"I've got your little dog!" said Stoat,
"Which in five minutes I will kill,
Unless you bring the certificate
Down to Whitchurch Mill!"

XLIV.

We punted the drunk bride to the mill pool
And a terrible sight we saw—
Stoat dangling the dog on a fishing rod
From the mill house upper floor!

XLV.

The pike was circling in the mill pool,
Doing its best to snatch it.
"Give me that certificate now!"
Cried Stoat, "Or I'll slacken off me ratchet!"

XLVI.

"We're *not* married!" came a voice from the Toll Bridge
And Susannah waved from afar.
"Gilly and I are going with Roger
To play tennis at Leamington Spa!"

XLVII.

I stooped and lifted the drunken bride's veil.
The situation got absurder.
For it was plain to see, by Roger's deceit,
Bunny had married the verger!

XLVIII.

"The certificate is annulled!" said the Rector.
Cried Stoat, "I can't believe I 'eard yer!
I always thought the good church taught
That one should marry a verger!"

XLIX.

"Thanks to you, Reverend Sir,
My inheritance is over.
You've ruined me! *C'est la vie!*
Say 'Goodbye' to Rover!"

L.

Stoat lowered the dog to the pike,
But the pike started to die—
For it was in the jaws of another pike,
Enormous – with only one eye.

LI.

With rod bent double and screaming reel,
Stoat slipped on a piece of dough
And, catapulted out of the mill house loft,
Crashed into the mill pool below!

LII.

He fell with such force on the larger pike,
The smaller pike leapt in our boat.
When the three-legged dog fell from its gob,
The Rector gave him a stroke.

LIII.

Meanwhile….
The one-eyed pike shot up Stoat's kilt,
Hungry and looking for dinner,
In the mistaken belief that what fluttered beneath
Was some sort of salmon spinner.

LIV.

The pike drove Stoat up the millrace.
The tartan hood sent it berserk.
As his head neared the blades of the mill wheel,
Stoat fished in his sock for his dirk.

LV.

Stoat planted the dirk amidships.
The pike's forward progress slowed.
Then he turned the fish by its handle
And the kilt became a drogue.

LVI.

When the millstream entered the tartan skirt,
Stoat shot down the race at a lick,
But the pike in tow wouldn't let go,
Like a bulldog with a stick!

LVII.

'Twas the Rector who towed Stoat ashore.
He took pity on a sinner.
He even offered to tend his wound
And cook him the pike for his dinner.

LVIII.

But the Doctor sent Stoat off to Reading,
Since his condition was grave and pathetic,
Where a vet and two surgeons removed
The pike, under a full anaesthetic.

LIX.

When we took the ledger to the vestry,
I discovered that the Rector'd misheard:
"The Boat Club land is *'glebe'* not *'grebe'*!" I cried,
"It belongs to *you*, not a waterbird!"

LX.

"I must tell Lady Stoat", said the Rector,
"And those tennis types, hale and hearty.
Sail me across to the tennis lawn,
Where they've come for the Betrothal Party."

LXI.

When the old Rector waded ashore,
He was greeted with jeers and scoffs.
"Here stood the Clubhouse of my friends,"
He said, "But you have made it a den of toffs!"

LXII.

"But I say unto you this…
This land is *glebe* land, *not* your land
And it's *theirs*, because it's *mine*
And, if you come here with your racquets or your oars,
I'll stick 'em where the sun don't shine!"

LXIII.

Then the Rector of St. Mary's
With righteous rage did quiver.
He cast off their boats, broke down their nets
And slung their balls into the river.

LXIV.

Lady Stoat was quite insulted,
But the Archdeacon said, "We'd better leave.
The Rector's well within his rights
If this land, indeed, is glebe!"

LXV.

The next day I borrowed a carthorse
And, with grappling hooks and chains,
We raised our clubhouse out of the depths,
Like a Phoenix from the Thames.

LXVI.

We put the clubhouse back in the field
And, to us, it seemed strangely bigger—
For it was lined throughout with streamer weed
And bonded by the mud of the river.

LXVII.

"I bequeath you this field", said the Rector,
"To you this land I do confer,
And may God bless you, and your Sailing Club,
And all who sail in her."

LXVIII.

We thanked the dear old Rector
And he gave us a courteous nod.
Then he wandered off to Pangbourne
For a pint, with his three-legged dog.

~ The End ~

Old Father's Source

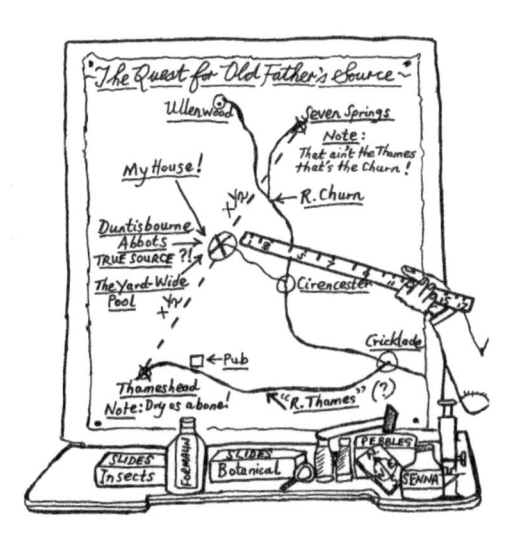

I.

When I was rusticated from Brasenose,
I was in need of employ quite badly.
So, from 1903, I taught Geography
At that well-known college called Radley.

II.

Geography's such a boring subject—
In the classroom you can almost smell it.
Alas, the head of "Geog.", was an enthusiast
By the name of Ernest Pellet.

III.

Ernest had once known Baden Powell.
He had a beard like a massive pelmet,
And he would teach his class in khaki shorts,
Wearing his old pith helmet.

IV.

Obsessed with the Quest for the Source of the Nile,
He'd drone on about John Speke much of the time,
Before turning to some matter like rubber from Melaka
Or Norwegian fish-canning in Trondheim.

V.

He had a passion for local Geography too,
And, much to the senior boys' mockery,
He studied the geology of the long-jump pit,
And made several maps of Matron's rockery.

VI.

One weekend, he took me to his Cotswold cottage,
Which was built out of soft stone, not brick,
And, dragging me into his study, he cried,
"Hey! Take a look at this, Dick!"

"Take a look at this, Dick!"

VII.

And there on his desk, was a map of the Thames—
He'd inked in the river's course—
And he'd written in red, at the top of the map,
"The Quest for 'Old Father's' Source".

VIII.

"This cross on the map marks the 'Thames Head Source',
Where you'll find no water", said Ern.
"This cross marks Cob'ley's Seven bubbling Springs,
But that ain't the Thames, that's the Churn!"

IX.

"The true source of the Thames is a mystery,
We're on the horns of a dilemma, do you see?
For the Thames Head Source is as dry as a bone
And from Seven Springs flows a tributary!"

X.

"But one night I cracked it with this ruler,
Which I keep wrapped in a hankie.
It is the very same lucky ruler
With which Nanny used to spank me!"

XI.

"From the Thames Head cross to Seven Springs cross,
This pencil line was carefully drawn
And, at the midway point betwixt the two,
I observed the legend… 'Duntisbourne'."

XII.

"This was my 'Eureka' moment, I felt
As if slapped on both cheeks with two haddocks,
For this cottage's very location
Is the village of Duntisbourne Abbots!"

XIII.

"Following the map, I went down Well Hill
Till I heard a faint tinkling sound, and there,
Not a hundred yards from me own front door,
'Ave a 'butchers', I'll show you what I found."

XIV.

Within a picket fence was a yard-wide pool.
Said Ernest, "I believe this to be spring-filled—
For it says so on that plaque attached to the fence,
Which was donated by the Church Women's Guild."

XV.

"The day after I discovered the pool,
It started pouring with rain
And I noticed the pool has an overflow,
Which runs off into that drain."

XVI.

"Nipping home, I found a ball in my outhouse,
Which appeared to be copper coated.
It was about the size of a grapefruit
And when luzzed in the pool it floated."

XVII.

"It sailed off over the overflow.
It was engulfed by that drain.
I never dreamed I'd ever see
My copper ball again!"

XVIII.

"Two weeks later, upstream of Abingdon,
I was taking a Botany class,
When a twinkle in the Thames caught my eye
And my copper ball sped past."

XIX.

"That ball confirmed my theory
With overwhelming force:
This little pool in Duntisbourne—
This is 'Old Father's' Source!"

XX.

"We'll go back to college and borrow a boat.
We'll row upstream on an expedition.
We'll prove my theory once and for all,
With the Warden of Radley's permission."

XXI.

We lingered awhile and stared in the pool
Then I saw something orange roll:
"That's Goldie, my goldfish", said Ernest,
"She's grown too big for her bowl".

XXII.

I agreed to go on the expedition—
How on earth could I refuse?
"Let's have a pint at *The Thames Head Inn*", said Ern,
"I want you to meet my 'Muse'".

XXIII.

When we entered the dingy Inn,
The Landlord gave us a dirty look.
He had a one-handed potman called Mungo,
Who was gathering pots on his hook.

XXIV.

Pictures of Old Father Thames adorned the walls—
The Landlord must have had a stencil.
He sold Thames Head water at two bob a throw,
Claiming it put lead in your pencil.

XXV.

The young barmaid pulled me a pint and said,
"I won't serve that bloke with a beard though—
I can't stand the way he ogles me.
I think he might well be a weirdo!"

XXVI.

"You are my Muse", Ernest enthused,
"Penelope of you I've grown so fond.
For you I'll find the true source of the Thames
And I will name it 'Penny Pond'."

XXVII.

"I'm going to prove your Landlord's a charlatan
And I'll do so with full propriety.
I've invited to Duntisbourne, next Friday morn,
The Chairman of the Geographic Society."

"Throw him out of my pub will yer Mungo!"

XXVIII.

"We'll see about that!" said the Landlord,
Draining a yard of ale at one go,
"I'll show him who's got the true source o' the Thames,
Throw him out of my pub will yer Mungo!"

XXIX.

Mungo swooped down from the top of the bar,
As a ruthless hawk from the sky hunts—
His left hand grabbed onto Ernest's beard.
His hook took hold in his 'Y' fronts.

XXX.

As Mungo dragged Ernest from the pub,
He certainly bought tears to his eyes.
When his hook pulled out of his underpants,
He created a new set of flies.

XXXI.

We cycled back to Duntisbourne
On Ernest's old tandem bike
And, showing me to my room,
He bade me a thoughtful "Goodnight".

XXXII.

"If you should wake up in the night, Dick,
And you feel desperate to 'strain the greens',
Go down to the end of my garden,
I've got one of these new *Crapper* latrines."

XXXIII.

"It was installed in a brick-built outhouse,
Which my sensibilities did appal—
So I made them remove the overflow pipe
And replace the brick with a dry-stone wall."

XXXIV.

"It's got a flushing chain, you know—
Oh, that really is the best bit!
It's fed by a spring not a main
And it's got it's very own cesspit!"
                    "Sleep well!"

XXXV.

I dreamt of a fast- flowing stream that night,
But woke when the dream had begun—
'Twas ten to two and I rushed to the loo,
In great need of a "number one"!

XXXVI.

The loo was so dark I had to sit down
To find the porcelain.
Then, all of a sudden, a man came in
And pulled the toilet chain.

XXXVII.

"Sorry to disturb you sir", said the yokel,
"But Mr. Pellet and I have got a system—
He pays me five bob a week to flush his bog,
'Cos there's an unexplained leak in the cistern."

XXXVIII.

When we got back to Radley College,
The Warden approved of our mission.
Next day, two Don's and a teacher's pet
Waved us off on our expedition.

XXXIX.

Five days later we reached Duntisbourne,
But both of us were nearly dead,
From giving each other piggy-backs
And dragging our boat like a sled.

XL.

We got to the pool with the picket fence,
But we couldn't see water for dust—
Or, to be more precise, a great pile of
Manure, with a concrete-hardened crust.

XLI.

Nearby in a puddle gasped Goldie,
Swimming round in little rings.
"This goldfish needs fresh water", said Ern,
"Let's take her to Seven Springs".

XLII

Ernest bore Goldie to Seven Springs,
In his helmet, then tried to float her.
She revived and shot up the Seventh Spring—
Like a carrot with an inboard motor.

XLIII.

'Twas dark as we left the grotto
And it was also spitting with rain.
Two carts appeared on the road above.
We heard the voice of the Landlord again.

XLIV.

"We've already dumped on Duntisbourne
Mungo, but it's worth the extra mileage,
To plug up the so called 'Seven Springs'
With these two carts o' rotten silage."

XLV.

We watched Mungo and the Landlord,
As they buried those Springs so pure,
Together with Goldie the Goldfish,
Under twenty tonnes of manure.

XLVI.

When we got back to Duntisbourne,
It was a dark and moonless night.
We both bumped into the picket fence
And so Ernest struck a light.

XLVII.

"I've dropped my specs, but I heard a plop",
Said Ern, "Oh Dick, it's such a thrill—
A tiny stream is refilling our pool.
Look! It's trickling down Well Hill!"

XLVIII.

We got on our knees when the match went out,
Using our hands to feel for the stream
And, inch by inch, we ascended the hill—
Towards the source of old Ernest's dream.

XLIX.

In the dark and wet, on hands and knees,
We felt like we'd scaled Ben Nevis,
When we reached a wall of Cotswold stone,
With water pouring through a crevice.

L.

Ernest prised out four stones with a file,
He carried for a toe-nail infection.
"Wait here", he said, "I am going inside—
This phenomenon needs inspection."

LI.

When he disappeared into that orifice,
I was fearful that he was in danger,
Till his voice echoed back, out o' the crack,
"I've discovered a water-filled chamber!"

LII.

"Water is pouring down the wall.
There's some sort of ancient font.
There's a hieroglyphic, me last match lit it,
More matches is what I want!"

LIII.

"All my weary life I've been on a Quest,
But I don't have to search anymore.
If this legend confirms it's 'Old Father's' Source,
I'll win Geography's *Palm d'Or*!"

LIV.

I crawled into the cave and struck a light—
My heart went pitter patter—
By its flickering light I read the words,
"Made by Thomas Crapper".

LV.

Then a door in the cave wall opened.
There stood the yokel in the morning fog.
"Me wife's been ill Mr. Pellet", he said,
"And I ain't had the time to flush your bog!"

LVI.

When the *Geog. Soc.* Chairman arrived, he said,
"That overhead cistern's developed a leak".
He lifted the lid with the loofah brush
And stood on the loo-paper nail to peep.

LVII.

"Someone's been tampering with this loo",
Said he, "I don't know who or what clot
Has taken away the copper ball,
Which should be attached to the stop cock!"

LVIII.

Then his foot slipped from the loo-paper nail.
He clung to the cistern with all his might.
He tore the tank and the chain from the wall
And completely severed the inflow pipe.

LIX.

The broken pipe became like a geyser.
Out of Ern's carsey a river did roll.
And out of that river leapt Goldie the Goldfish,
Who ended up in the lavatory bowl.

LX.

"This is most interesting", said the Chairman,
"You will hear my views, Pellet, in due course—
For tonight, at *The Thames Head Inn*, I'll give
My final verdict on 'Old Father's' Source."

LXI.

When we arrived at the Inn that evening,
The Landlord gave Ern a sarcastic nod.
"Here's the bloke who thought the source was a pond",
He joked, "But it turned out to be his bog!"

LXII.

"Let me be the judge of 'Old Father's' Source",
Said the Chairman, "For I've considered each source on merit—
I've studied Thames Head Source and Seven Springs
And the spring found by Mr. Ernest Pellet."

LXIII.

"At Seven Springs I found no water—
Just some sort of silage dump.
The Thames Head water was from the canal—
This Landlord had used a pump."

LXIV.

"So, I can only conclude from this
And the other evidence I have,
That the true source of the River Thames
Is…Mr. Ernest Pellet's Lav.!"

LXV.

But then, at the moment of his triumph,
I turned and blurted out to Ern,
"If we lost the goldfish at Seven Springs,
The River in your lav.'s the Churn".

LXVI.

This hit him like a body blow,
As did the barmaid's scornful smile.
"I'm going off to Ullenwood",
He said, "Dick, I might be awhile".

LXVII.

Next day I went to Ullenwood
And found Ernest sleeping by a stream.
I'd never seen him rest before—
He looked so calm and so serene.

LXVIII.

He was usually so dead earnest,
But when I knelt by his side
He really was dead Ernest—
For my friend Ernest had died.

LXIX.

Ernest had died of a broken heart,
Exhaustion and hypothermia
And due to the fact that his khaki shorts
Had badly strangled his hernia.

LXX.

When I sat down by my friend to cry,
By that brook in that glade remote,
I saw his hand was pointing upstream
And it held a little crumpled note.

LXXI.

The note read: "I leave you one last theory Dick,
For my life has run its course,
I now think this Ullenwood arm of the Churn
Might well be the 'Old Father's' Source!"

LXXII.

These days I'm head of "Geog." at Radley.
I have a beard like a massive pelmet
And I teach my class about Ernest's Quest,
While proudly wearing his old pith helmet.

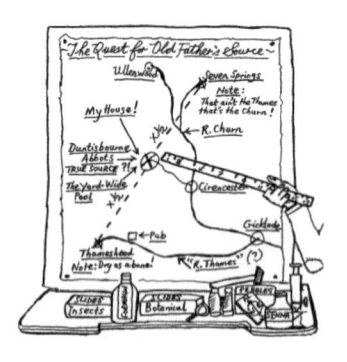

~ The End ~

The Dames of Wallingford

I.

My former Rector, the Reverend Wright-Jesse
Of Wallingford on Thames,
Liked nothing better than playing the parts,
In Pantomimes, of Dames.

II.

The Rector of St. Mary-the-More with Peter
Rarely tended to his flock,
Unless they were in the audience
And he was in a frock.

III.

He'd say: "If I write 'em a boring sermon,
They never ever thank me,
But I'm showered with flowers for 'alf an hour
When I play Window Twanky!"

IV.

"For, when I played Titania in 'The Dream'
At school, 'twas a triumph ne'er forgotten.
I upstaged the leading Fairy – Puck—
And got many more laughs than Bottom!"

V.

When the Rector played in a pantomime
He'd a rather large hidden agenda:
He'd got the hots for the Principal Boy,
Who was a thigh-slapping lass called Brenda.

VI.

As Puss in Boots she'd stolen his heart—
She was so gorgeous and golly-goshy.
But, playing Aladdin, she'd dashed his hopes
When she "got off" with Wishy Washy.

VII.

After his umpteenth curtain call,
The Rector's elation had turned to rage
When he found Wishy Washy with Brenda,
Canoodling round the back of the stage.

VIII.

What incited the Rector the most,
To the point where he couldn't endure it,
Was that he'd given the role of Twanky's son
To none other than Eric, his curate.

IX.

When Eric left Wallingford under a cloud
How Brenda had mourned for her fella,
While the Rector wrote a script to win her back,
As Prince Charming in *Cinderella*.

X.

I first met Wright-Jesse the next Michaelmas.
I was recovering from pleurisy.
I'd been sent by the Bishop to Wallingford
To fill the vacancy in the Curacy.

XI.

I'd mugged up on Anglican Canon Law,
I'd bought my sermon on the fishes and loaves,
And I'd been to *Wippell's* of Tufton Street
To buy some clerical Oxford brogues.

XII.

When I reached Wallingford Rectory,
I could barely walk down the path.
Those size 10 brogues were killing my toes—
I should have bought 10½!

XIII.

My eyes went up to the Rectory attic
When my shoes made me blaspheme and grimace
And, in the window, I spied an old lady,
With a ghostly, luminous, smiling face.

XIV.

A young maid named Lucinda answered the door
And my heart missed a beat with a jolt.
She was poor and plain, even boyish in looks,
But I was struck by the old thunderbolt!

XV.

I must confess I'd lived a sheltered life till then.
My two brushes with love were antiquarian:
I'd once winked at a Sunday School teacher called Gwen
And glimpsed the ankle of our college librarian.

XVI.

As Lucinda led me to Wright-Jesse's room,
I believed I'd met the love of my life.
Though slim and demure, she was oozing allure.
She'd make a marvellous clergyman's wife.

XVII.

In the study I met a formidable Dame,
Sporting a blue rinse and beehive hairpiece.
She had a colossal bosom, an ugly "boat"
And more war paint than the wife of Cochise!

XVIII.

"I've come for an interview Madam", I said,
"Are you the Reverend Wright-Jesse's mother?"
"No! I'm Dr. Wright-Jesse of Pembroke College—
I'm the Rector of Wallingford's brother!"

XIX.

"I'm staying at Wallingford till Christmas.
My students in Oxford can lump it.
My brother tells me his pantomime cast
Is packed with eligible 'crumpet'!"

XX.

The Rector stormed in and shouted at me,
"If you're Mr. Bell my new curate, you're late!"
From his desk he took a strawberry-blonde wig
And slammed it on his parsonical pate.

XXI.

"Get back to the kitchen, you lazy girl!"
He shrieked, bundling Lucinda out of the door.
"She's as common as muck!" his brother squeaked,
"You just can't get the staff anymore!"

XXII.

"Don't cry Lucinda!" I called to the maid,
"You'll always have me for your friend.
I will lend you a hand in the kitchen
And 'Love conquers all', in the end."

"I'm giving you the rôle of Buttons!"

XXIII.

"You've got the job Mr. Bell", said Wright-Jesse,
"But you'll have to shave off those 'Muttons',
For, when we star as the Ugly Sisters,
I'm giving you the rôle of Buttons!"

XXIV.

"Darling Brenda says she'll play Prince Charming,
But she's made a condition that hinders—
She's taken a shine to my dozy new maid
And wants her to play the part of Cinders."

XXV.

"I said 'yes', but she's banned from rehearsal,
Because she's far too common for that.
You can hear her lines in the kitchen
When we adjourn to the bar of the *C.A.T.*"

XXVI.

"Mr. Bell you can take all my services—
I find the tedium of Church quite alarming,
But don't err like my last curate Eric—
Keep your mits off my Brenda, Prince Charming!"

XXVII.

"Preach what you like from my pulpit,
I can tell you hold Puseyite views,
I can see you agree with my brother 'n' me
For we all wear the same Oxford shoes."

XXVIII.

That Autumn, I took all Wright-Jesse's services,
So that he could start his rehearsals sooner
And lure Brenda and friends to *The Coachmakers Arms*
For cashew nuts and sweet sherry by the schooner.

XXIX.

Each night I rehearsed with Lucinda alone,
Followed by a spam sandwich and *Ludo*
And, as I heard her lines, she'd hear me sigh
And, when she asked me why, I'd say: "You know".

XXX.

But she didn't know how much I adored her
And that I spied on her more than I oughter—
For when she went to bed, she'd sneak out instead
And was a secretive "midnight walker".

XXXI.

One night I followed her down the pitch black lane
That leads to Wallingford Castle ruins.
She met Brenda on top of the old keep's mott
And I just couldn't believe their doings.

XXXII.

They sang and they danced in the moonlight
Till Lucinda lost one of her shoes
And, when Brenda returned it, they kissed,
In a way I felt girls shouldn't do.

XXXIII.

Lucinda went down to the ruins each night
And I didn't know how to protect her.
"That kid's lost her moral compass", I thought,
But I dare not tell the Rector.

XXXIV.

By Christmas week, this emotional state
Had quite cured my constipation,
When Deeney came to the Rectory
With the Party Invitation.

XXXV.

"Reverend Sirs", said the dandified Butler,
"Brenda's father invites you to a post-panto Ball,
On Christmas Eve at his mansion,
Which stands near the old castle wall."

XXXVI.

"He wants to find Brenda a husband
And preferably a well-heeled cleric,
For he's sick to death of her moping at home
And droning on about that ex-curate Eric."

XXXVII.

"He wants you to come along in costume
With the whole cast of *Cinderella*—
You've more chance of a dance if you're dressed as birds
'Cos Brenda'll be dressed as a fella!"

XXXVIII.

"I bagsy the first dance with Brenda!"
Cried the Rector, going all gleeful and smirky,
"But you *won't* be going Lucinda",
He said, "You can stay at home and stuff my turkey!"

XXXIX.

"And be at St. Peter's by midnight",
He barked, "Given your purport to believe.
You can take my Midnight Mass Mr. Bell—
I'm otherwise engaged this Christmas Eve!"

XL.

On Christmas Eve, the folk of Wallingford
Came in droves to the Masonic Hall.
The Rector planned to steal the show
And to propose, to Brenda, at the post-panto Ball.

XLI.

But the Ugly Sisters performed poorly—
They were overly camp and lewd.
They were both too fresh with Prince Charming
And, at the end of the show, they were booed.

XLII.

Lucinda, as Cinders, was star of the show.
Oh, how that humble maid rose to the occasion!
Her duet with Prince Charming brought the house down
And received a ten-minute standing ovation.

XLIII.

Lucinda's love for the Prince seemed so real,
I felt her affection for me had wilted.
When she said "Goodbye Buttons", I wept in the wings,
Feeling all alone and completely jilted.

XLIV.

When I got Lucinda back to the Rectory,
She went all maudlin and melodramatic.
"If only I could go to the Ball", she sobbed,
"And you shall go!" came a voice from the attic.

XLV.

'Twas the old lady I'd seen who called from the loft:
"Come here dear, I won't be alarmin' yer.
You can borrow this gown for the ball tonight—
'Twas the Rector's when he played Titania."

XLVI.

The dress fitted well, but the shoes were too small,
Which the old girl kept boxed in rows,
So Lucinda borrowed a posh pair of mine—
Viz. me clerical Oxford brogues.

XLVII.

In the ball gown and mask she looked stunning
As I led her to the Mansion by moonlight,
"I'll meet you in the lane by the ruins", I said,
"We must rendezvous just afore midnight".

XLVIII.

"You must get to St. Peter's church by twelve
And make sure the Church Warden observes yer.
If you don't, the Rector's bound to find out
'Cos you'll be grassed up by old Gittings the verger."

XLIX.

But, when I got back to the ruins at ten to twelve,
There was no sign of Lucinda at all.
Then I heard her voice ring from the tow-path—
Had she been abducted after the ball?

L.

I spied her in a skiff drifting down the Thames,
I called out, but she didn't see or hear me,
For she was singing a duet with a handsome Prince,
Namely Brenda, rowed by dandy butler Deeney.

LI.

I rushed onto the bridge as the skiff approached
And something left by workmen renewed my hope
That I might still pluck Lucinda from that boat,
For they'd left behind a derrick with a pulley and a rope.

LII.

Alas! the Ugly Sisters arrived in a boat,
Shouting, "Princey don't leave us in the lurch!"
"Grab hold of me rope Lucinda", I cried,
"For I must haul you up in time for Church!"

LIII.

I pulled her up as the Church clock struck,
The Prince clung to one foot in despair.
The Sisters tried to hit her with shoes,
Which they flung as she hung in mid-air.

LIV.

Lucinda *must* be at Mass on time,
So I took a drastic action—
Holding the rope, I jumped from the bridge
To gain some extra traction.

The Prince clung to one foot in despair.

LV.

Lucinda shot up and off as I came down,
But Brenda was holding her shoe in such sorrow,
That I fed the rope back through the block
And I started hauling her up to follow.

LVI.

The Sisters grabbed her rope to pull her back
And I started going up again.
I stopped going up when Deeney pulled on mine
With a dandy's might and main.

LVII.

Then Brenda made a most decisive move—
She switched from one rope to the other:
Up shot the Sisters, for we t'other three
Outweighed the Rector and his brother.

LVIII.

When the Wright-Jesses crashed into the pulley,
Brenda and Deeney let go of their rope,
So that I shot up and the Sisters came down
Towards their awaiting boat.

LIX.

The Ugly Sisters descended at speed
Like two drag-clad *d(e)i ex machina*
And, whilst I ascended and went off to Church,
They sank their own boat after smashin' her.

LX.

Brenda came to the Rectory on Boxing Day,
With her father, who announced the news
That his daughter would marry the owner
Of one of a pair of shoes.

LXI.

The Wright-Jesses got highly excited,
Indeed, they were almost hysterical.
For the shoe was like the ones they threw—
It was a *Wippell's* Oxford Clerical.

LXII.

The shoe was too small for them and me,
For I need a ten and a half,
But when Lucinda asked to try it on
They said, "You're 'aving a laugh!"

LXIII.

When the shoe fitted Lucinda,
Brenda gave her a passionate hug
And the maid's hair came off in the process,
For she turned out to be wearing a "rug"!

LXIV.

For Lucinda was not a humble maid,
Nor the girl who had swung from my derrick—
To our surprise, she was a bloke in disguise,
The Rector's ex-curate Eric!

LXV.

Wright-Jesse took the moral high ground
And with sanctimony he told him off:
"You've been deceitful, immoral and kinky", he said,
"You must be defrocked for disgracing your cloth!"

LXVI.

"How dare you chastise Eric!" I said,
"For Rector, 'tis you who have deceived us—
You preferred, to your shame, to camp it up as a dame,
When you should have taught us the Gospel of Jesus."

LXVII.

"You never impressed me", said Brenda,
"Your obsession with panto's a neurosis—
For you cannot sing, you over-act
And, in the love scenes, you've halitosis!"

LXVIII.

"But I was star of 'The Dream' at school", he wept,
"If only my House Master was here today.
He got sacked when we went to that Godalming pub
And Puck drowned in the River Wey."

"Don't cry", said the old lady from the attic.

LXIX.

"Don't cry!" said the old lady from the attic,
"I am, and always was your patron.
When they sacked me, I came back to the school,
Disguised as the Charterhouse Matron!"

LXX.

"When I retired, you took me in—
You've been to me like a son."
And he put his arm around Wright-Jesse,
Who said, "Daddy!" and sucked his thumb.

And how do I feel about all this?

LXXI.

Like Buttons, I'm left with a broken heart,
Due to unrequited love for a Cinderella,
But it was worse for me, as she turned out to be
A cleric, called Eric, a fella.

LXXII.

So I married my love in the end,
Without laying a finger upon her—
For I married Eric to Brenda,
In front of *three* Matrons of Honour!

LXXIII.

I was Rector of Wallingford for thirty years,
But, when I left, none of the Thespians missed me,
For, by then they'd formed the *Sinodun Players*,
Under the presidency of *Dame* Agatha Christie.

~ The End ~

The Blue Dahlia

I.

My wife was courtier to Princess Alexandra—
"Woman o' the Bedchamber" and by no means a fool
And I was courtier to Prince Bertie o' Wales—
His "Man of the Privy"-"Groom of the Royal Stool".

II.

But when Prince Bertie lost his appendix,
The Princess asked me to leave his loo.
She imported a bidet from Denmark,
With matching "doughnut" in Danish blue.

III.

When Alexandra was Queen, the palace régime
Increased in its Danish flavour
And I was retired with my wife to Hampton Court,
Granted rooms there by "Grace and Favour".

IV.

My wife hated the life at Hampton Court—
The day trippers made such a din,
Our rooms were cold and damp and every night
We got haunted by Anne Boleyn!

V.

How she pined for our time at Sandringham,
Especially for the fresh vegetable pottage
She'd made from the veg. that Prince Bertie grew,
As taught by his Dad, on the Isle, at Swiss Cottage.

VI.

"Remember King Edward's potatoes", she'd say,
"You could pop 'em in the mouth and melt 'em.
All we get here is roach from the Thames
And those tasteless carrots from Feltham."

VII.

After several years, one morning in May,
I was walking Bonzo, our aging pug,
When I met a lady resident in a courtyard
And noticed she was carrying a trug.

VIII.

"I'm sick to death of topiary!" she said,
"Fountains, formal beds and azaleas.
So I've nabbed meself a patch near Pond Gardens
And I've planted a trugful of Dahlias!"

IX.

"I believe you're Bishop Creighton's widow", I said,
"I'm Sir Reginald Knollys, please call me Reg.
I wonder if you've any room by your Dahlias, Ma'am,
For me to grow my wife a few veg.?"

X.

"There is room to the right of my pom-poms",
She said, "We'll become the palliest of partners—
With my stunning blooms and your luscious legumes,
We'll outshine those glum palace gardeners."

XI.

Mrs. Creighton and me made a wonderful team,
She got my seeds "Tested" from *Carter's*,
I made frames for her plants with bamboo canes
And she mulched my young "cukes" and tomatoes.

XII.

Mrs. Creighton would hoe between my rows
And I'd gather her weeds in my barrow,
And sometimes I'd grease her Dahlia stems,
While she moistened and polished my marrow.

XIII.

But our horticultural idyll
Met a rude end in July,
When a bumptious palace official
Drove up in a horse-drawn fly.

XIV.

It was Lancelot Bloom the Royal Gardener
And he was very angry indeed.
At his side was his know-all Nurseryman,
Who went by the name of Doug Seed.

XV.

"I'll have no vulgar blooms in Pond Gardens!"
He cried and gave us a filthy scowl,
Before beheading twenty Ball Dahlias
With a swipe of his gold-plated trowel.

XVI.

"Remove all these vegetables Mr. Seed!"
He said, "I want them all gone by nine.
Rot 'em in my deepest compost heap
And feed 'em to the Hampton Court Vine!"

XVII.

"You 'Grace 'n' Favour' types are all alike:
You think your own manure don't smell,
But I am the Royal Gardener here,
Commissioned by Queen Alexandra as well."

XVIII.

"She wants me to grow her a rose,
Bluer than the bluest bluebell,
So copies can be sold for her charity,
Made of paper for the lapel."

XIX.

"The Queen esteems my gardening skill—
That's why she gave me the commission,
But she wants the general public involved
So she's made it a competition."

XX.

"On September the First the Queen will come
To judge my blooms against those of amateurs.
Mr. Seed will receive these at the Lion Gate—
Oh yes!... with *Weedol* and secateurs!"

XXI.

"Now get out of my garden the pair of you.
If I find another Dahlia here I'll snip it.
Get yourselves an allotment in Bushey Park
And, while you are at it, a cloth cap and whippet!"

XXII.

The following Sunday morning,
After Chapel, poached eggs and haddocks,
Mrs. Creighton and I got our own plot
On the allotments known as "Royal Paddocks".

XXIII.

The Chairman was none other than Doug Seed's brother
And he allotted our plot without mercy.
It had honey-fungus and snails, bindweed and mare's tails
And a grumpy old neighbour called Percy.

XXIV.

When we said "Good Morning" to Percy,
He was reluctant to give us a look.
After two weeks, we made a breakthrough,
When he answered our greeting with "Woop!"

XXV.

Gathering buckets of fallow deer dung
Was one of Percy's maudlin joys,
But he'd knelt in the musk of a rutting stag
Which gave a nasty niff to his corduroys.

XXVI.

When he went off on his trike to get the dung,
You'd hear one hell of a din,
For, when rutting stags got wind of his cords,
They would try to rut with him.

XXVII.

Mrs. Creighton took a shine to Percy—
She even borrowed his wellies,
And she began to spend a lot of time
Behind his rustic trellis.

XXVIII.

One morning I became alarmed
By Mrs. Creighton's calls:
"Come look behind the trellis Reg—
Percy's only grown *blue* balls!"

XXIX.

Percy was sixty-one, he lived with his Mum,
He'd known disappointments and failures,
But, behind that trellis, in fallow deer dung,
He'd grown truly blue Ball Dahlias!

XXX.

"These could win the Queen's competition", I said,
But Doug Seed's brother wasn't impressed at all.
"No flowers allowed on the allotments!" he said
And flung Percy's tubers over the wall.

XXXI.

T'other side of the wall lies Bushey Park,
Where Percy recovered his tubers next morn,
But, whilst loading them into a barrow,
His trousers were smelt by a stag called "Big Horn".

XXXII.

When "Big Horn" charged, Percy stood firm,
Like a Roman resisting the Vandals.
Behind his barrow, he locked horns with the stag,
Using the wheelbarrow's handles.

XXXIII.

Trapped between barrow and wall, he climbed a tree,
By a series of complex manoeuvres,
But his trousers got caught on the barrow's rim
And they fell off and covered his tubers.

XXXIV.

Driven mad by the musk on Percy's legs'
Erstwhile corduroy regalias,
The stag smashed his barrow, tossed his cords in the air
And started to eat his Dahlias.

XXXV.

Just one node remained. I watched from the wall.
The stag opened his gob. I cried, "No!"
Then onto Bushey Park cricket pitch
There wandered an in-season doe.

XXXVI.

The rampant stag lost all interest in food—
With one whiff of the doe, he was gone.
Percy shot down the tree, rescued his node
And put his trousers back on.

XXXVII.

The surviving node was oval in shape,
The size of a beef tomato.
Percy hid it among his *Pentland Crowns*,
Disguised as a seed potato.

XXXVIII.

On the day of the flower competition,
Percy mounted his trike at noon.
He was going to show the Queen his node
And we would vouch for its bloom.

XXXIX.

But a plot holder had spilled the beans.
The realisation hit me,
When the Chairman emerged from behind a shed,
With the entire Allotment Committee.

XL.

"No flowers on the Allotments!" said the Chairman,
"And that means no bulbs 'n' tubers 'n' all!"
And he snatched the node from Mrs. Creighton's trug
And slung it over Bushey Park's wall.

XLI.

A cricketer was searching the long grass,
On the other side of the wall.
"I'm awarding a six", the umpire cried,
"If you fail to find that ball!"

XLII.

When the fielder found Percy's node,
He tossed it to the bowler,
Who bowled it at a fearsome pace—
He really turned his shoulder.

XLIII.

The Dahlia node spun through the air
And came off the pitch unsmoothly—
It hit the batsman's box and bails
And got him out, with a double googly!

XLIV.

Hampton Wick Cricket Club
Were playing the local Foundry
And the next artisan who came to the crease
Whacked Percy's tuber over the boundary.

XLV.

Percy pedalled his trike with all his might,
Although it was hot and muggy.
Mrs. Creighton and I rode behind
In a home-made soap box buggy.

XLVI.

We shouted to a distant lady,
"Catch our Dahlia if you can!"
But she didn't try and it fell from the sky,
Right into her baby's pram.

XLVII.

When the baby threw it out of his pram,
A retriever gave a bark
And took the node to Diana Pond,
On the other side of the Park.

XLVIII.

The dog's master took it and threw it away—
He didn't want Fido to keep it.
And a carrion crow flew off with the node
Onto Diana's gold head to eat it.

XLIX.

The crow dropped the node into the pond,
Which wasn't very clever.
It was engulfed at once by a leather carp,
Known as "Heather the Leather"!

L.

Mrs. Creighton and I were devastated
And in sorrow our heads we hung.
"We must start again", said Percy—
"Let's look in that glade for some dung."

LI.

And suddenly, under a chestnut tree,
We found a bloom that couldn't be bluer—
It was the most perfect Blue Ball Dahlia,
Growing out of a stag's manure!

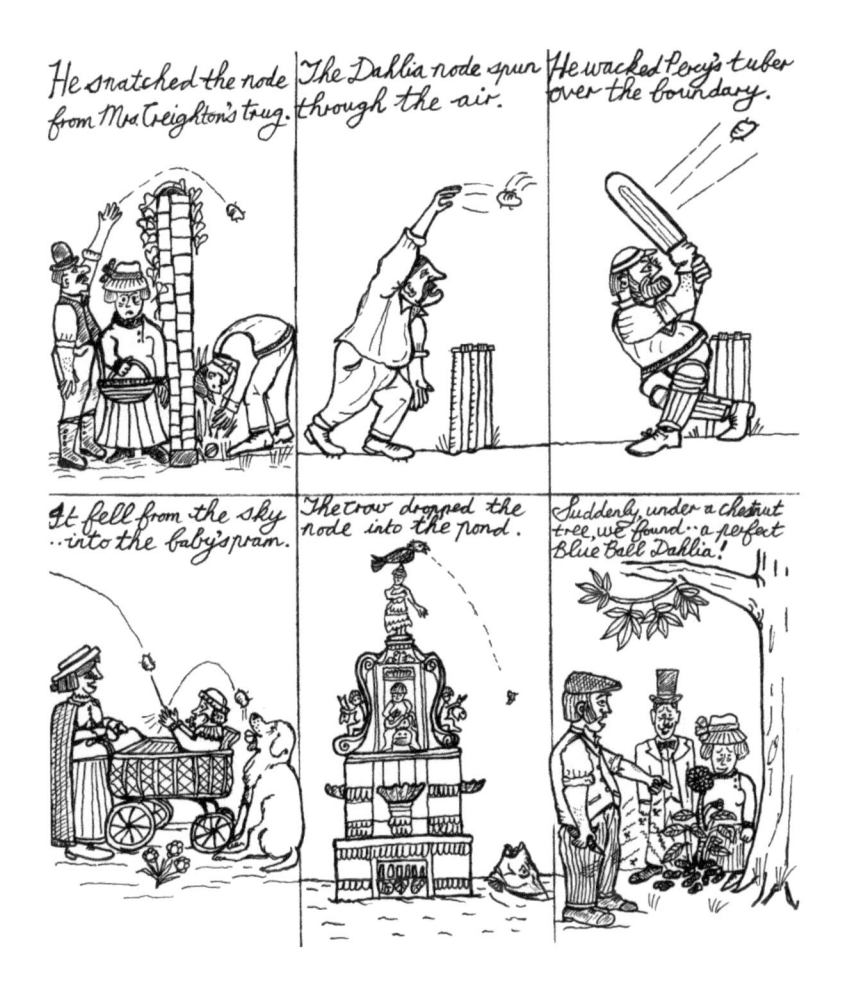

He snatched the node from Mrs Creighton's trug.

The Dahlia node spun through the air.

He wacked Percy's tuber over the boundary.

It fell from the sky ...into the baby's pram.

The crow dropped the node into the pond.

Suddenly, under a chestnut tree, we found... a perfect Blue Ball Dahlia!

LII.

More epic than the voyage of Captain Cook,
When he sailed round the World to Australia,
Had been the voyage round a stag's digestive tract
Taken by Percy's Ball Dahlia!

LIII.

We took the bloom on the trike to the Lion Gate,
But we heard a bellowing noise—
"Big Horn" the stag was in hot pursuit—
He'd smelt Percy's corduroys!

LIV.

We ran inside *The King's Arms* pub.
The chasing stag let rip a rutting roar,
When Percy locked him in the saloon,
By wedging his dibber under the door!

LV.

At last we arrived at the exhibition tent.
We took in our flower, but promptly ran away,
For Lancelot Bloom and Doug Seed were within
Drenching the exhibits with *Scot's Co. Weedol* spray!

LVI.

When the Royal Gardener saw the Blue Dahlia,
Jealousy from his eyeballs did blaze,
And he shouted these words to his Nurseryman,
As we ran off to hide in the Maze.

LVII.

"I want that Blue Dahlia to meet an end
More tragic than Massenet's *Werther*!
Follow them into Hampton Court Maze
On that massive machine called 'Big Bertha'!"

LVIII.

Driven by steam – a hedgecutting machine—
"Big Bertha" was an absolute whopper!
She could buzz-cut the Maze in half an hour,
Shooting the offcuts into her hopper!

LIX.

Cowering with our flower the midst of the Maze,
We *didn't* feel safe as houses.
The stag had escaped and followed "Bertha" in,
Getting scent of Percy's trousers.

LX.

With Bertha just a hedge away,
We really had to stop her.
So Percy let his trousers drop—
Over the hedge-top – into "Bertha's" hopper.

LXI.

When the stag attacked the hopper,
Doug Seed fended him off with a rake.
When its handle went through the steering wheel,
"Bertha" turned right, before he could brake.

LXII.

Doug Seed fell onto the stag's antlers,
While we three ran out of the Maze,
Following the driverless hedge-cutter,
Which carved us a massive swathe.

LXIII.

In the Garden of the Great Fountain,
Sat the Queen with a flower to her nose.
"I've grown it for you", said Lancelot Bloom,
"The World's first and only blue rose!"

LXIV.

"The amateur gardeners failed", he said,
"Apart from those people behind me—
They've grown a dreadful Blue Dahlia,
Which I'm sure you'll find far too 'Cor Blimey'!"

LXV.

The Queen looked down towards the Maze.
When she saw us she started to choke,
For Percy was fighting the stag in his underpants,
Using his trews as a matador's cloak!

LXVI.

When his braces got caught on the antlers,
They served as a catapult—
The brace buttons burst and the cords were launched,
At the speed of a thunderbolt!

LXVII.

The trousers hit the Royal Gardener,
His head was swathed in corduroy fronds
And the stag charged and butted him, with his blue rose,
Into the biggest of Hampton Court's ponds!

His braces got caught on the antlers!

LXVIII.

His rose wasn't blue when he emerged from the pond.
He must have painted its petals with ink.
He handed the Queen a droopy thing,
Which looked small, pathetic and pink.

LXIX.

"I'm not using that for my charity",
Said the Queen, "It would be an absolute failure.
It wouldn't sell and it isn't blue.
I'd rather use their Dahlia!"

LXX.

"But tell that little man to go,
His appearance quite affronts!
It's most obscene to meet the Queen
In an ol' pair of white 'Y'- fronts!"

LXXI.

"You're not having my Blue Dahlia",
Said Percy, "Because it's the only one.
I'm taking it back to Teddington
And giving it to my Mum!"

LXXII.

"Well, this silly pink rose'll have to do",
Said Alexandra, "My charity starts so soon,
But I'm not impressed Royal Gardener—
I dub thee, 'Incapability Bloom'."

LXXIII.

"You've treated my 'G. & F.' Residents
In a way that's far from kind.
I grant them their own flowerbed,
Down by the Hampton Court Vine."

LXXIV.

And this is why…..
If you visit the gardens of Hampton Court,
Down near the Orangery,
A wonderful bed of Dahlias,
To this very day, you'll see.

LXXV.

They grow in all shapes and sizes,
But you'll never find a blue one,
For no one there has Percy's skill,
Nor grows his nodes in deer dung.

LXXVI.

And as for Percy, I bought him some trousers
And took them to his mother's cottage
And she gave me a hamper of his freshest veg.,
So my wife could, *finally*, make her pottage.

~ The End ~

The Goblets and the Gondolier

I.

In my youth I was something of an oarsman.
In fact, I rowed Bow in the Oxford boat,
When Lord Desborough rowed at Number Four
And our Stroke was Lord Bunny Stoat.

II.

In the year Eighteen Seventy Seven,
Stoat tried to fix the Varsity Race
And, with chum Roger Smoothly, got "sent down"
From Oxford in total disgrace.

III.

Several years later at Pangbourne,
A mishap befell Stoat most awful:
A one-eyed pike swam up his kilt
And grabbed hold of his "Oh-be-joyful"!

IV.

You wouldn't wish that upon any chap,
Although there seemed a certain justice to me,
Besides, a vet and a surgeon removed the pike
And the local Vicar cooked it for Stoat for his tea.

V.

After that, I heard no more of Bunny Stoat
And I rarely saw Lord Desborough,
For I moved downstream to Henley-on-Thames,
When I married my dear wife Deborah.

VI.

I retired from all competitive rowing,
But, you know, it didn't seem to matter,
For I became Honorary Member of *Leander Club*
And a steward at Henley Regatta.

VII.

I was granted an honour in 1902,
Which normally only a snob gets—
The Chairman of Stewards made me Umpire
Of the pair-oar *Silver Goblets*.

VIII.

But on the day of the race the Chairman seemed grave,
Dishevelled and without his club tie on,
For dreadful rumours had reached his tent,
From the saloon bar of *The Red Lion*.

IX.

"Someone's made a bet on the *Goblets*", he said,
"He's got a hundred to one on the Brasenose boat,
Winning before Trinity reach Fawley Court.
That someone is…..Lord Bunny Stoat!"

X.

"Make sure this doesn't happen Alan", he said,
"For you are my starter and referee.
Stoat mustn't again defame our sport
And, besides, I've got a 'pony' on Trinity!"

XI.

"Don't give Brasenose the Berkshire bank.
If they win the draw – make 'em toss.
They've got a weak crew: vetran Smoothly, R.
And Tom's boy – Edwards-Moss."

XII.

I went down by launch to Temple Island,
Where the *Goblets* starts, in weather bright 'n' sunny,
The Trinity Crew were moored to the downstream end,
Eating crumpets with Granchester honey.

XIII.

Tied beside was the Brasenose Boat,
But no sign of her crew, which was funny,
And I began to worry that "Smoothly, R."
Was that infamous chum of Bunny.

XIV.

I went into the Temple's Etruscan room
And discovered whisky and lemonade.
So I went up on the roof and looked down on the lawn,
From behind the classical colonnade.

XV.

I saw Edwards-Moss approach two men,
Who were sharing a whisky flask—
Bunny Stoat was one of 'em and, atop his head,
He sported a snorkel and a diver's mask!

XVI.

"By cheating you destroyed my father",
Cried Moss, "I won't let it happen again.
Stoat, don't tie a rope to the Trinity Boat,
But, 'Play up and play the game!'"

XVII.

"You'll do as I say", said Stoat
And pulled out a snub-nosed "shooter".
But Edwards-Moss was a Boxing Blue
And punched him on the end of his "hooter".

XVIII.

A fight ensued on the Temple Lawn,
Which continued on the river's beach
Till Moss' *Tomoe nage* Judo throw
Sent Stoat flying…..into the Henley Reach.

XIX.

When Stoat sank out of sight,
I sensed it wasn't the end of our troubles,
For I think I glimpsed a snorkel pipe
And an upstream trail of bubbles!

XX.

The Trinity Crew went off at a furious pace,
Then slowed and Brasenose began to catch 'em,
'Cos, by means of a rope tied to their keel,
A half-sunk barge was attached to 'em!

XXI.

When Brasenose Boat went past Trinity,
Edwards-Moss got up on his knees,
Stopped rowing and cried, "This is cheating"
And they turned one eighty degrees.

XXII.

The Brasenose Bow, Smoothly, got to his feet
And started to fight with his Stroke,
Until young Edwards-Moss knocked him out,
With a blow of his oar that then broke.

XXIII.

The Trinity Boat went past
And the half-sunk barge drew level
And out of its stagnant waters rose
Lord Bunny Stoat like the Devil!

XXIV.

He knocked Edwards-Moss overboard,
With a swipe of his snorkel's hose,
Took out the barge's drain-plugs
And leapt aboard Brasenose.

XXV.

As the barge sank down in the river,
Trinity rowed more slowly,
Till it hit the bed and stopped 'em dead,
Ten yards downstream of Fawley.

XXVI.

"This must be against the rules", I thought,
So I approached in my umpire's boat
And attempted to stop the race,
By shouting these words to Stoat:

XXVII.

"A pair can't row when one's 'sparko',
As if he's been drinking stingo.
Your mate lies astern with knees in the air—
He's totally 'legs akimbo'!"

XXVIII.

"I've often sported in Venice", cried Stoat,
"Where Venetian courtesans frolic,
Where gondoliers scull with one oar in a crutch
Called a *'forcola'* not a 'rowlock'."

XXIX.

"So leave me alone and let me row,
I do not wish to talk to yer!"
And, with just one oar, Stoat started to scull,
With Roger Smoothly's crotch as his *forcola*.

XXX.

Roger came round at the finish line
And he didn't seem annoyed.
He was thrilled they'd won the *Goblets*—
The strange sculling he'd rather enjoyed.

With just one oar, Stout started to scull.

XXXI.

Stoat and Smoothly were carried shoulder high
By Brasenosians, to *The Red Lion* they went,
Where they all drank champagne from the *Goblets*
They'd nicked from the Stewards' Tent.

XXXII.

The Chairman of the Stewards marched into *The Lion*,
With bumptious rage he did quiver,
For they'd smashed the gates on Henley Bridge
And chucked them into the river.

XXXIII.

"You're disqualified from the *Goblets,* Stoat!"
He railed, "I consider your style a foul.
You've sculled like a garlic-scoffing foreigner,
On some dingy Venetian canal!"

XXXIV.

"You can keep your *Silver Goblets*", cried Stoat,
"I know you're a Cantab man.
You'll find 'em in *The Red Lion* 'carsey',
First cubicle, lavatory pan!"

XXXV.

"In September I go to Venice
To marry Contessa Veronica.
I plan to complete in the Gondoliers' Race
Known as 'Regatta Historica'."

XXXVI.

"I love *'La Dolce Vita'*,
Bardolino and *gelato*.
Like chum Roger I've always been
Something of an *Inglese Italianato*."

XXXVII.

I went home with Deborah after the race,
But felt strange and all of a dither,
For I found her talking with Roger Smoothly,
In *The Little Angel* pub by the river.

XXXVIII.

"Take me to Venice", she said next day,
"For its literary works intrigue me.
I love the prose of Giacomo Casanove
And the satires of Carlo Goldini."

XXXIX.

Two months later we arrived in Paris—
Deborah wore the most revealing dress.
I'd booked two tickets for Venice,
On the famous *Orient Express*.

XL.

We had a first-class sleeper compartment
And, for me, one of its extra perks
Was that the W.C. was right next door—
You see, I've a dodgy water works.

XLI.

Deborah acted strangely at dinner—
She used napkins to write little notes.
The waiter took them to the end of the car,
Where I thought I heard a voice like Stoat's.

XLII

As Deborah undressed in our sleeper,
I decided to visit the loo.
Locked within, I heard Stoat's voice
And Roger Smoothly's too.

XLIII.

"I'm going to win the Regatta", said Stoat,
"And I really couldn't be happier.
I've placed a ten million lire bet,
Borrowed from a bank called 'The Mafia'."

XLIV.

"Don Alfonso, who runs the bank,
Says he can fix the race.
He controls the Gondoliers' Union,
So they'll all scull at a slower pace."

XLV.

"His top gondolier will partner me—
His name is Corleone Tony.
He lives on a diet of raw veal shins
And his Mamma's macaroni."

XLVI.

"I want you to chaperone the Contessa—
You're better than me in the saddle,
Particularly since the Pangbourne pike
Got hold of my 'wedding tackle'!"

XLVII.

"Leave it to me," said Roger,
With an air of happy resignation,
"I'm meeting another lady now,
In her sleeper for an assignation!"

XLVIII.

Stoat then kicked the lavatory door,
"Get out! It's ten minutes I've waited!
You should take a dose of syrup o' figs,
If you are really that constipated!"

XLIX.

I climbed out of the lavatory window,
I clung to the side of the thundering express,
But, when I went into the next door window,
I found Roger in a state of undress.

L.

I must have gone in the wrong window,
Which I thought was rather weird,
So I climbed into the next compartment
And got into bed with a bloke with a beard!

LI.

Going back to the first compartment,
I found that Roger had gone
And Deborah was looking rather flushed,
Still putting her nightdress on.

LII.

We arrived at the *Danieli* in Venice,
And the next day Deborah went missing.
I glimpsed Roger spooning in a gondola,
But it was a Contessa he was kissing.

LIII.

As I searched for my wife in Venice,
My head fair spinning with fears,
I met a gondolier called Luigi,
Behind the *Fenici*, in floods of tears.

LIV.

"My father defied Don Alfonso",
He wept, "He refused to throw the race.
When he said we'd win the *Storica*,
They said: 'Shut uppa your face!'"

LV.

"They killed his Italian whippet,
They put its head on the end of his bed,
They threw him off the *Camponile,*
Mio padre é morto....'e isa dead!"

LVI.

"Cheer up, Luigi!" I said to him,
"I've already grown quite find of yer,
Show me what to do and I'll crew for you,
In your two-man racing gondola!"

LVII.

The race got off at a furious pace,
Then the gondoliers did their duty,
They slowed in front of "The Bridge of Sighs",
So that Stoat's boat led at *Salute.*

LVIII.

But, I'm proud to say, we took the lead,
When we reached *Palazzo Moro,*
Luigi poured his rage into his oar
And his pent-up filial sorrow.

LIX.

As we neared the turning point,
I observed an oncoming water bus.
Stoat pulled a pistol and shot me—
The bullet hit my surgical truss.

LX.

The bullet ricocheted away,
Which for me was very handy,
But it hit Luigi in the arm
And he fell in the *Canale Grande*!

LXI.

As Stoat approached from behind,
I saw Roger in a passing gondola,
Escorting a lady with a huge ice cream
And looking rather fond of her.

LXII.

I snatched the ice cream from her hand
And the gondolier came aboard to assist,
For Stoat and Tony were now alongside—
What could I do to resist?

LXIII.

I was armed with only an ice cream,
But the result was truly amazin'—
As Stoat sculled by, I stabbed him in the eye
With a *Cornetto* of rum and raisin!

I was armed with only an ice cream.

LXIV.

To steer a two-man gondola at speed
Is a skill that's awfully tricky—
It's much harder to do when one of the crew
Has an eyeful of *Mr Whippy*!

LXV.

The ice cream got stuck between Bunny's eye
And one of his trade-mark monocles.
In the water bus' path, his craft was cut in half
And sank, like a couple of coracles!

LXVI.

The Doge presented the cup when we won the race,
Sitting on his barge he looked furious.
The young gondolier, who'd assisted me,
Gave me a kiss, which was curious.

LXVII.

I recognised his floral Cologne,
Of garlic he didn't reek,
And, when he withdrew from our embrace,
He left his moustache upon my cheek.

LXVIII.

It was Deborah my wife in disguise—
She said she'd been foolish, God bless her!
She'd become aware of Roger's intentions,
By spying on him and the Contessa.

LXIX.

We went back to our hotel by gondola,
Our oarsman wore a mask which was queer.
Then, he took it off and pulled a gun—
Bunny Stoat was our gondolier!

LXX.

"I'm sure you two won't grass me up",
He said, "And bring Brasenose great disgrace.
I'll take your cup to my Bookie at home
As proof I won the race."

LXXI.

He snatched the cup and turned the craft,
He was heading for the *Ca' d'Oro*,
For the Doge's barge was in hot pursuit
And a boat of men with violin cases followed.

LXXII.

"*Arrivederci* Don Alfonso!"
Cried Stoat, "You half-witted Italian!
You won't catch the Champion Gondolier
In a Doge's boat, built like a galleon!"

LXXIII.

Stoat took a sharp right at *Cannaregio,*
Where Deborah and I leapt ashore.
We managed to seize the cup
And Bunny broke his oar.

LXXIV.

With half an oar he paddled under *Guglie* bridge,
The Doge's barge was too wide to follow,
But the boat of men with violins was waiting there—
They'd nipped round the *Canale Colombola.*

LXXV.

"I am the Godfather!" Don Alfonso cried from the bridge,
"And you have gone against my wishes!"
He took a spherical bomb from his Doge's cap,
"Tonight you sleep with the fishes!"
[Narrator mimes throwing the bomb]

" Tonight you sleep with the fishes ! "

LXXVI.

Stoat swatted the bomb with his broken oar,
A sort of "reverse sweep"-cum-backhand from *Queen's*,
And the bomb went over his shoulder
And blew the violinists' boat to smithereens.

LXXVII.

"I won't be holidaying here again", cried Stoat,
"To tell you the truth it smells.
And you ain't my Godfather anyway—
He's Canon Twitting of Bath and Wells!"

LXXVIII.

And as for the Venetian Trophy……
It was sold at a Henley auction room
To Guy Nickalls' Dad, who's far from hard up,
And today it's presented with the *Goblets*
Known as the *Nickalls' Challenge Cup*.

LXXIX.

These days my wife and I go away Henley Week,
To Walton, where we have a pretty riverside hut.
We take our lunch each day at *The Old Crown* pub,
And then row slowly back down dear Lord
Desborough's Cut.

~ The End ~

The Last Monologue of Weybridge

I.

I'm a Chartered Accountant by profession,
Which for my Boat Club is rather handy,
For I audit their annual accounts,
My name is… Sandy Spanley.

II.

I was obsessed with Chartered Accountancy,
I would audit my grocery bills whilst sleeping,
And I had two doors fitted to my bookcase,
For the sake of "Double Entry" bookkeeping.

III.

I had a distinguished career in the city –
I survived mergers which seemed unending,
And, because I ran The Sports and Social Club,
I survived all the subsequent "ethnic cleansing".

IV.

I ended up as the accountant in a public school,
My salary reduced but a smidgen.
The Bursar there was a Brigadier,
Who used a rifle to thin out the pigeon.

V.

I retired to spend more time at my Boat Club,
On the Thames at Weybridge, which I adore,
And I bought myself a meandering cruiser
Off Old Omnibus, the Past Commodore.

VI.

The deposition of dear Old Omnibus
Was one of our Club's gravest mistakes—
We got a keen new Commodore, name o' Peter Pratt,
Who wanted to move us to Littleton Lakes.

VII.

A former Commodore of *Thamesis Club*,
Peter Pratt was pals with the local Mayor—
They were both in property development
And the same Lodge, being both "On the Square".

VIII.

Things came to a head at a meeting,
In the back bar of *The Crown*—
Peter Pratt gave the Committee a roasting,
Whilst pacing up and down.

IX.

"You call yourself a Sailing Club",
He raged, "I find this an absolute joke!"
He swallowed his gin and his face went puce,
When a peanut lodged in his throat.

X.

"You've barely two dozen members,
Plus Pete's two dogs and their bone,
You're a disgrace to Weybridge, you rarely sail,
And most of you hail from Addlestone!"

XI.

"Your annual regatta's pathetic!
Does anyone get my message?
There's not enough wind at Dorney to sail,
So you do a sort of nautical dressage."

XII.

"Secretary Bill Tray wins every race,
There's never been another,
And he doesn't sail anyway—
He moves by wiggling his rudder!"

XIII.

"If we get more members and give back our field,
The Mayor'll let us have Littleton Lakes.
I'm determined to make you a Sailing Club
And I know the two measures it takes."

XIV.

"*One*: Treasurer N. 'Ron' Purtis is coming back,
Mainly 'cos he's a mate of me.
He's replacing honest Hattie Tray—
I want our accounts kept 'creatively'!"

XV.

"*Two*: Your membership's in terminal decline.
You sit there and look agog,
But I've worked out the very cause of this—
It's Jim Larter's Monologue!"

XVI.

"Every year at the Boat Club Dinner,
For well over a decade or more,
You've scared off prospective new members
By giving the floor to that crashing bore!"

XVII.

"No one can stand his Monologues,
Old members do their best to avoid 'em,
They're all about Oxford and public schools,
When he went to Secondary Modern in Croydon!"

XVIII.

"So I'm asking you Sandy Spanley,
Since you are Jim Larter's only friend,
To tell him there'll be no Monologue this year
And his Monologue-writing must end!"

XIX.

"But Jim's already written one", I protested,
"It will break his heart what you request!"
And I made a swift exit to *The Old Crown* loos—
I'd had several pints of Best.

XX.

I was washing my hands in the sink,
Soothing a whitlow on my cuticle,
When I was tapped on the back by Peter Pratt
And a flush sounded out in the cubicle.

XXI.

N. "Ron" Purtis emerged and grabbed my hand.
His grip was that of a mason.
He and Peter Pratt lifted me up
And sat me down in the basin.

XXII.

"Where does Jim Larter keep his script?"
They cried, "You must answer our enquiry!"
"He's bringing it on my cruiser next week",
I said, "We go for a recce at Newark Priory".

"Where does Jim Larter keep his script?"

XXIII.

"We're going to moor on the Wey near Pyrford—
Jim's written a ghost story this year.
He wants to visit the Priory after dark,
So he can sample the atmosphere."

XXIV.

"Make sure he leaves his script aboard",
Said Peter Pratt, "There's a lay-by close by for cars.
Let us know what time you'll leave the boat,
You can phone us from *The Seven Stars*."

XXV.

"And, if you dare to disobey", said N."Ron",
"Your professional status you risk.
For I will report to the I.C.A.
You signed off all my withdrawals marked 'Misc.'!"

XXVI.

"I'll do as you say!" I bleated—
I complied much more than I oughter—
N."Ron" had stuck the tap in me pocket
And was filling it up with cold water.

XXVII.

I was unable to stay in the bar that night
For one of Omnibus' customary beanos,
For the water from the tap had created a map
Of India in the lap of my chinos!

XXVIII.

Next weekend I rowed Jim 'n' his wife
To *Leander IV* – my heart was full o' fear.
Jim boarded my cruiser, script in hand,
And we set off from Coulson's Weir.

XXIX.

We brought a map, a torch and sandwiches
And fresh water in an old jerry can.
We also brought Jim's mother-in-law, Pearl,
Whose first boyfriend was a Native American!

XXX.

As we neared Thames Lock to enter the Wey,
We did so with some trepidation,
For a twenty stone lock keeper, called "Big Gord",
Ruled the gates of the Navigation.

XXXI.

As we entered the holding chamber,
He cried: "Come up here you twerp!
No boat enters *or leaves* me Navigation,
Without the c'rrect paperwork!"

XXXII.

There's a little cupboard on my cruiser,
Next to the *Thetford* bog,
And I stored Gord's paperwork safely there,
Alongside the "Captain's Log".

XXXIII.

Jim's mother-in-law said she loved my boat,
And in her youth she'd been a beauty.
After a couple of "snowballs" at Pyrford Lock,
She turned a little bit fruity!

XXXIV.

"I'll sleep on deck, you can have my bunk",
I said, as we moored in Walsham Meadow,
But to no avail: "Let's 'top and tail'",
Said she, "You cheeky little fellow!"

XXXV.

"We'll all go to *The Seven Stars*", said Jim,
"And then on to the Priory when they close the door".
"You can count me out!" said an irate Pearl,
"Me bedtime's always ten – o - four!"

XXXVI.

Before we set off for the pub,
I hid the script of Jim's Monologue,
By swapping covers with Big Gord's papers,
In the cupboard by the "Captain's Log".

XXXVII.

I locked the cupboard door with a key,
And, before we went away,
I hung it round the neck of sleeping Pearl,
Down her nylon negligee.

XXXVIII.

I phoned Peter Pratt from *The Seven Stars*.
It was an act of most dreadful betrayal,
While Jim and his wife sat in a booth,
Attacking pork scratchings 'n' *Gale's Ale*.

XXXIX.

We reached the Priory ruins at midnight—
Jim was convinced he saw a ghost pass.
What worried me more were torchlights I saw,
Coming down the River Wey's towpath.

XL.

Hastening to where the Abbey Stream joins the Wey,
I'll never forget what I saw—
Peter Pratt and N. "Ron" were being repelled,
From the poop deck of *Leander IV*.

XLI.

Jim's mother-in-law launched a fierce attack,
Before either of 'em could hit her—
She whacked 'em both with the "Captain's Log",
And put the boot in with a *C. & A.* slipper!

XLII

Peter Pratt was hit in the eye with a *Mills & Boon*!
His feet in Pearl's knitting got caught!
He fell and pulled N. "Ron" over the side,
Into the Wey's frogspawn and pennywort!

Jim's Mother-in-Law launched a fierce attack!

XLIII.

As Pratt ran away up the bank,
His left foot in a cow pat slipped,
And out of his hand, into the Wey,
Flew the pages of Jim's precious script.

XLIV.

What a relief when we re-boarded *Leander*,
For safe in the cupboard by the "Captain's Log",
Still hidden in the covers of Gord's paperwork,
I found the script of Jim's Monologue!

XLV.

But when I drove the cruiser into Thames Lock,
And Jim, mooring, was not aboard,
His wife, Penny, made a dreadful mistake:
She handed Jim's script to Big Gord.

XLVI.

I ran up to his Lockkeeper's Cottage,
But he'd already started to lock it,
And I could see he'd rammed Jim's Monologue,
In his snug-fit trousers' back pocket.

XLVII.

"My office closed ten seconds ago!"
Said Gord, "So don't come to this door again,
Until 9.30 am tomorrow,
Because 'A refusal sometimes offends'!"

XLVIII.

Jim was frantic at the loss of his script—
For its safety he prayed to the Lord!
Next day Gord's wife came to the door,
And we asked, "Can we see Big Gord?"

XLIX.

It was one of those questions one regrets,
Almost as soon as one asks it,
For she took us into the sitting room
And there was Big Gord ......*in a casket*!

L.

"He's too heavy for Mitty's to get down the path",
She wept – with grief she was almost choking.
"Tomorrow they'll bear him by barge down the Wey
And stick him in their hearse near Woking."

LI.

We were unable to retrieve Jim's script,
'Neath Gord's backside, it just wouldn't bend,
So, next day, we followed Mitty's hearse by car,
Till they picked up Gord's body at Send.

LII.

"I've got a plan", said Jim,
"In my darts team there's a chap called Clem—
He sports a massive 'comb-over',
And he's the furnace-man at Woking Crem."

LIII.

"There's an ante room in the Crem.
The coffin goes to when they wind it through.
Here, Clem will retrieve my Monologue,
Afore he sends Gord up the flue!"

LIV.

But we were in for a shock at Woking,
For when the hearse reached St. John's—
It drove past the Crem. to Jacob's Wells
And then, on and on beyond!

LV.

We caught up at Portsmouth Cathedral,
The hearse was parked on the quay,
Within we heard 'em sing the hymn,
"For those in peril on the sea".

LVI.

A naval chaplain gave the eulogy—
In Gord's nautical life he rejoiced.
Then they loaded Gord onto a tug boat,
With the help of a docker's hoist.

LVII.

When they buried Gord's coffin at sea,
It popped up and started to float,
So Jim lassoed it with a rod and line,
For we'd followed in a mackerel boat.

LVIII.

But Jim Larter's beloved Monologue,
Alas! was lost in a tragic moment,
When the Isle of Wight Ferry hit Gord's box
And it sank to the bottom of the Solent!

LIX.

It was the day of the Boat Club Dinner,
At *The Warren Lodge Hotel*—
Sir John the Mayor sat with Peter Pratt
And the Lady Mayoress as well.

LX.

She wore a mink coat 'neath her Mayoress' chain,
She had a feminine laugh like a chirrup,
She had a hat with a veil 'n' a hair-style so large
It could only have been a "syrup".

LXI.

"The Mayor will speak first", said Peter Pratt,
"This year there's no silly poems,
For Jim Larter's latest Monologue
Now rests with 'Davey Jones'!"

LXII.

"*Au contraire*", said Nell and Stu Tavey,
"Jim Larter's on his way by boat—
To read *all* his *other* Monologues,
Since he knows 'em not by rote."

LXIII.

"Lock all the doors, N. 'Ron'",
Said Pratt, as the Mayor got to his feet,
"Here are the keys to my speedboat—
Intercept Larter from Shepperton Creek!"

LXIV.

"Your future lies at Littleton Lakes", began the Mayor—
"Rubbish!" shouted his wife, who appeared to be sloshed,
"You and Peter Pratt are after their field,
To build luxury flats!" she scoffed.

LXV.

"You're drunk again Betty!" said the Mayor
To his wife, "Be quiet till my speech is over!"
But Betty sprang up and smacked him in the mouth
With the remains of her mango *Pavlova*!

LXVI.

The Lady Mayoress then collapsed—
She must have had too much booze—
The Mayor dragged her out by her ankles
And left her in the gentlemen's loos.
(He did at least open the window of the loo,
To let a little bit of fresh air through.)

LXVII.

It was almost time for my financial report.
I went to the hotel bar for a Stingo,
And I saw N."Ron" in a speedboat ramming Jim,
As I looked through the river-view window!

LXVIII.

Poor Jim's boat was completely wrecked
And into the icy Thames he slipped,
I watched his little head bobbing about
As he gathered pages of his floating script!

LXIX.

When I got up to do my report,
There was a smattering of polite applause—
I glimpsed Jim, with a script, in wet underwear
Passing by the locked French doors.

LXX.

The Mayoress shot out of the Gents during my speech—
From a gin bottle she did swig!
She leapt on the table and removed her furs—
It was Jim Larter in Betty's wig!

LXXI.

When Jim held aloft his dripping script,
Peter Pratt punched him in the gob,
But *maître d'*, Malcolm, came to Jim's aid—
He was a big fan of The Monologue!

LXXII.

Malc whacked Peter Pratt with a peppermill!
He took out N. "Ron" with a cream filled bun!
And he locked 'em both, with Sir John the Mayor,
In the room he'd reserved for Jim Larter's Mum!

LXXIII.

"I'll tell you the tale of Sir Peregrine Foukes",
(Said Jim), "I was once his fag at Eton—
I used to iron his shirts and butter his scones
And when I didn't I was soundly beaten!"

LXXIV.

(From this point on it all went wrong—
Jim got himself really kerfuffled,

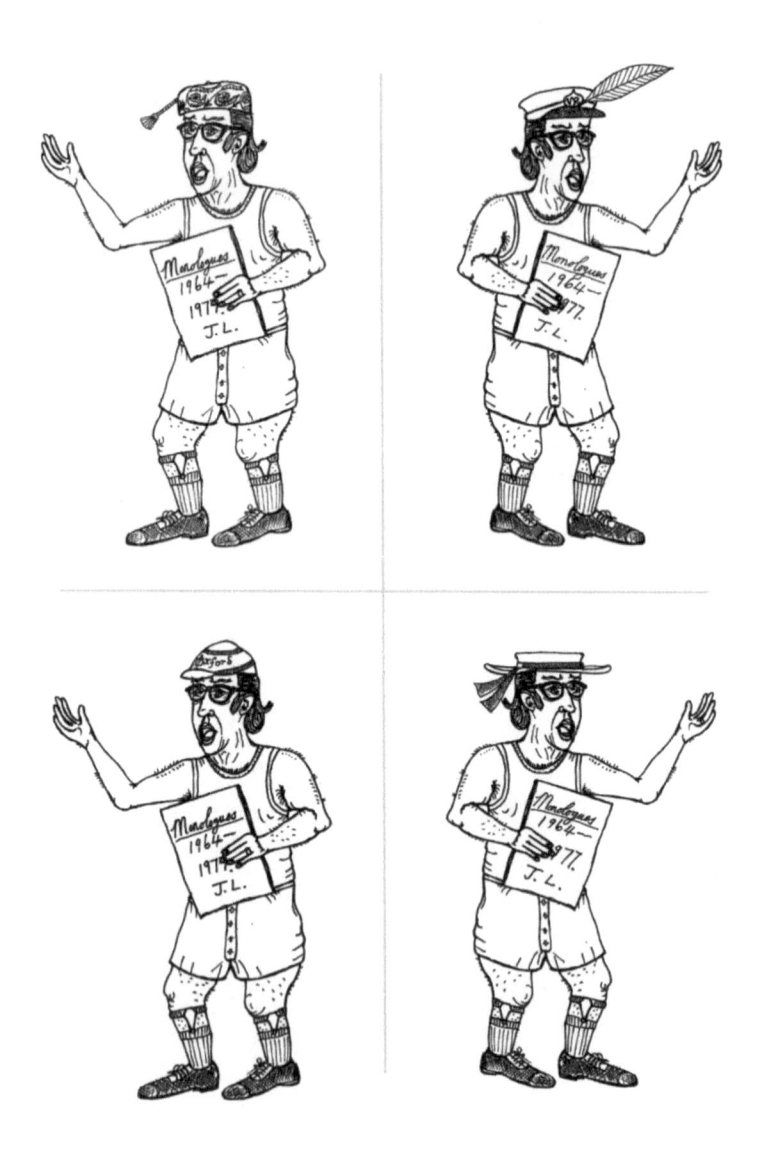

As bits of old Monologues fell from his lips
From the wet pages he'd randomly shuffled!)

LXXV.

"Er… And this is the tragedy of Sir Hugh-Jampton Johns,
Who was once the Keeper of the Queen's Royal Swans…

…A one-eyed pike swam up his kilt,
Hungry and looking for dinner,
In the mistaken belief that what fluttered beneath
Was some sort of salmon spinner! …

…He was armed with only an ice cream,
But the result was truly amazin',
As he shot by, he stabbed him in the eye
With a *Cornetto* of rum and raisin! …

…And *suddenly*, under a chestnut tree,
He found a bloom that couldn't be bluer—
It was the most perfect *Blue Ball Dahlia*,
Growing out of a stag's manure! …

…He prised out four stones with a file,
He carried for his toe-nail infection,
'Wait here', he said, 'I'm going inside,
This phenomenon needs inspection!'…

…He went down beneath the stage,
Crawling through the dirt,
Until he popped out of a little trap door,
Beneath the Soprano's skirt! …

…'You've never impressed me', said Brenda,
'Your obsession with panto's a neurosis—
For you cannot sing, you overact,
And, in the love scenes, you've halitosis!' …

… He poured himself a pint of gin.
He looked for ice and lemon.
He lifted down the old fruit bowl—
There was only half a melon.
With bleary eyes he spied the bird—
He thought it was a lemon!
And Johnny Jones' sparrow,
In yellow painted trim,
Was cast away like a piece of fruit
And *drowned* in a pint of gin!"

LXXVI.

Truth and fiction then blurred in a manner absurd,
For Betty's gin had made Jim quite lairy,
With extended hand, he approached the bar,
Where Malcolm kept a canary.

LXXVII.

I feared for the life of that little bird,
For Jim the bar was mounting—
So I bashed my friend over the nut
With the ledger I use for accounting!

LXXVIII.

I thought I'd killed Jim at first—
Yet no one chose to applaud him,
When he got back on his feet to give us a verse,
Even more pathetic and maudlin!

LXXIX.

"And that's the way it's always been
Since the World's inception—
Our golden dreams are washed away,
Our heaven-sent dreams of perfection!"

LXXX.

He burst into tears and his wife stood up,
And she gave him a tender kiss—
Then she said to him: "I love you Jim,
But *you don't have to keep doing this*!"
(…..and then he shut up and sat down.)

LXXXI.

Dear Old Omnibus called for three cheers!
And the Committee, with help from Mayoress Betty,
Debagged Peter Pratt, N. "Ron" and Mayor Sir John,
And slung 'em off the *Warren Lodge* jetty!

LXXXII.

And as for Jim Larter…
Rob Avagander has taught him to sail,
And old Vic Cutler's teaching him to play bridge,
He's happier now and membership's increased—
For that was: "*The Last Monologue of Weybridge*!"

LXXXIII.

And as for me, Sandy Spanley…
I married Jim Larter's mother-in-law,
Which was the best idea I've had—
For now I'm not only Jim's best mate,
I suppose I'm also his Dad!

~ The End ~

Performance Notes

In General

The earlier monologues were shorter and normally only required a hat. Over the years they have become more complicated and involve a few basic props and the occasional hat or jacket change, which I will outline below. It remains even more important to have a sober prompter. Act out the moments of high drama, but work out in advance when you are going to breathe. There were occasions when the audience began to fear for my health. I have devised a very effective way of learning a monologue in four weeks. Learn the first half in week one, and the second half in week two – you must finish a performance as confidently as you start. In week three put the two halves together. In week four polish, and work out your actions in front of the bedroom mirror. On the morning before the performance, recite the monologue three times. Then go to the dinner, eat it, drink several glasses of wine and perform the monologue *before* the raffle. Good places for daily rehearsal are: walking the dog, in the bath, behind your fish counter (-or similar, but warn your colleagues, "It's that time of year"), driving to and from work. Warning: if you are in heavy traffic, behind or alongside a white van driver, do not practise in an animated fashion – it might lead to a misunderstanding. Good luck!

The Parson of Pangbourne's Pike

The narrator is the Commodore of Pangbourne Sailing Club. Wear a navy blue Breton style sailing cap with a homemade "P.S.C." badge fixed to the front. Wear a Cornish style fisherman's smock and stick on large grey mutton-chop whiskers. Lord Bunny Stoat (see *The Oxford Cox*) speaks confidently and quickly, affecting a foppish "teapot" stance, which he reverses after each statement. When the pike goes up Stoat's kilt in the mill pool, and drives him towards the mill race etc. *act* out the drama, but do remember to breathe (verses 53 to 57). If not, it takes most of the dénouement to recover.

Old Father's Source

The narrator is a geography teacher, who ends up as a disciple of the hero, Ernest Pellet (see verse 72). You should wear a tweed jacket with pens in the top pocket, a tweed tie and a pith helmet. Shorts are optional. You should stick on a chin-strap beard, with no moustache, but be warned, mine fell off. The barmaid (verse 25), the landlord (verses 27 and 61) and the yokel (verses 37 and 55) should speak in standard, "country bumpkin" voices, even a Bristolian "Ah – Jim Lad" would suffice. When the *Geog. Soc.* Chairman stands on the loo-paper nail (verse 56), stand on a chair, and jump off when his foot slips (verse 58). The pathos of Ernest's death is enhanced if you take a crumpled piece of paper from your hand (verse 70) and pretend to read (verse 71).

The Dames of Wallingford

For this monologue, dress as a vicar, with dog-collar, but have a pantomime dame's wig to hand. It is essential that this is easy to put on and to remove swiftly: so an upright "beehive" style is better than a wig with long, flowing tresses. Put the wig on at the end of verse 20. Take the wig off at the end of verse 27. The wig should be put on for verse 63 and then removed. It should be put on again for verse 69 and then removed. The most dramatic section of the monologue involves Wallingford Bridge and the derrick. As well as miming all the rope pulling and shoe throwing, it helps to get up and down on a chair. Get on the chair (verse 53); jump off the chair (verse 54); get on the chair (verse 56); get down from the chair (verse 57); rapidly mount the chair (half way through verse 58 – "So that I shot up") and then dismount ("The sisters came down") and repeat in the next verse (59). Mount the chair on "Whilst I ascended" and do a two footed jump from the chair on "They sank their own boat after smashin' her". NB: I have performed twelve monologues, and taken a total of six prompts. Four prompts occurred in *The Dames of Wallingford*. The breathless exertion of the derrick scene, and the wig changing, may have had something to do with it. I may have had too much wine. The Past Commodore's wife noticed and voiced disappointment at my memory lapses, which I found painful to accept. So, bear this in mind.

The Blue Dahlia

The narrator is a retired courtier. Wear a velvet smoking jacket, with white shirt and black bow tie, and stick on a dapper moustache. When you get your own allotment (verse 22), you become poshly "cor blimey". Remove the smoking jacket, don a Harris Tweed hacking jacket and a cloth cap of the "cheese cutter" variety. Doug Seed's brother (verse 40) should speak in a 1970s style Shop Steward/Police Constable voice. The cricket scene (verses 42 to 45) should be acted out in convincing fashion, the hedge-cutting machine "Big Bertha" requires mechanical flailing arm movements (verse 58) and the launching of Percy's corduroys from the deer's antlers should be made clear by your actions (verses 65 to 67).

The Goblets and the Gondolier

Begin the monologue wearing a striped Henley blazer and traditional rowing cap with a dapper moustache. Conceal what is beneath by wearing a white silk stole. Bunny Stoat returns, so affect once more the quick confident speech, with the foppish teapot stance, particularly verses 28 to 29 and 34 to 36. *Note*: in verse 38, Deborah gets the names of two famous Venetians wrong. It is, of course, Giacomo Casanova and Carlo Goldoni. The mistake assists our rhyme scheme, but it stems from Deborah's pretentiousness. She isn't interested in Venetian literature at all – she just fancies Roger Smoothly! (see also *The Oxford Cox*). Don't forget to mime climbing in and out of the windows of *The Orient Express* (verses 49 to 51). Luigi (verses 54 to 55) should have a classic "cod-Italian" accent, ladened with emotion. By contrast, verse 56 is delivered in a decidedly stiff-upper-lipped, Anglo Saxon manner. At this point, take off your Henley blazer, revealing a striped gondolier shirt beneath. This got a cheer, when I did so. Cast aside your rowing cap, and don a Venetian boater. (The genuine articles can be bought, at great expense, beneath the Rialto Bridge, on the market side, but tourist versions will suffice.) It serves the drama, and wakes the audience up, if you produce and fire a loud cap gun in verse 59. In verse 61, get your prompter, or your wife, to hold a *Cornetto* ice cream aloft. In verse 62, take it from their hand ("I snatched the ice cream from her hand"). Use the ice cream as a prop in verses 63 to 65, and then hand it back to your prompter or wife, after "trade-mark monocles". Get your prompter/wife to eat it, or distribute as they see fit. (You will need to bring it to the dinner in a cool box.) For verse 68, try to procure a Venetian mask on a stick, which can be held in front of the face. In verse 75, you are not wearing a Doge's cap, so mime removing the bomb from inside your boater.

The Last Monologue of Weybridge

Sandy Spanley is a Chartered Accountant, so wear a latex bald head wig. Ideally, you should sport a grey beard, but, as these are liable to fall off mid-performance, a grey "Old Git" style stick-on moustache will suffice. Wear a double-breasted navy blue blazer, preferably with a badge, a cravat and beige chinos, with sailing shoes. (This monologue is set in the late 1970s.) Big Gord, the lock-keeper, should speak in a 1970s Shop Steward/Police Constable voice (verses 31 and 47). Pearl, Jim's mother-in-law, should be played (verse 34) with a pantomime dame voice, as should Mayoress Betty (verse 64) who is also drunk. Jim's "kerfuffled" Last Monologue (verses 73 to 79) should be acted out as if Jim is cold, wet, confused, drunk (he's been at Betty's gin), desperate to perform (to the point where "truth and fiction are blurred") and ultimately, pathetic. He should change hats eight times, as follows. Begin (verse 73) by wearing a smoking hat. At the onset of verse 75, this is exchanged for a Swan Upper's hat (a "Thames Admiral" boating cap adorned with a swan, or goose feather, at a jaunty angle). This is switched to a retro-Oxford rowing cap, just before the line, "A one-eyed pike shot up his kilt". The Gondolier's boater is donned before the line, "He was armed with only an ice cream", and this is switched for a cloth cap to deliver the line,

"And suddenly under a chestnut tree". A pith helmet is put on before the line, "He prised out four stones" and this is, in turn, replaced by a bee-hive wig for, "'You've never impressed me', said Brenda". After the word "halitosis", the wig is removed and the smoking hat is placed on your head for the rest of *The Last Monologue*. [An attentive reader may ask: "Given that Jim has been in the Thames, and arrives at *The Warren Lodge Hotel* in his wet underwear with pages of his script retrieved from the river, how does he have seven hats?" The answer is simple. His good wife, Penny, brought them to the hotel by car.] In verse 80, for the first time in any of the monologues, another voice is heard. Get your wife or prompter to stand up and kiss you, and then to say: "I love you, Jim, but you don't have to keep doing this". Then sit down, and get up to recite the last three stanzas (verses 81 to 83).

The Topography of the Monologues

When you perform a monologue about the River Thames, it really helps to have in your mind's eye, a picture of the location of which you speak. The earlier monologues were set alongside stretches of the Thames with which I was already familiar – Weybridge, Chertsey, Windsor, Cliveden, etc. As my stories have moved further upriver, topographical research has been necessary, and this has led to most enjoyable weekends by the Thames, in the Spring, with my dear wife, Jenny. I go away with the germ of an idea for a good yarn in my head, and when I arrive at the location where I plan to set it, I have often found that the truth imitates my fiction. I will give three examples.

We visited Pangbourne and Whitchurch prior to writing *The Parson of Pangbourne's Pike*. I had the idea of a disputed piece of land whereupon the sailing club had their hut. On crossing the toll bridge, I noticed a spit of grass between the mill pool and the lock cut. There was a workman working on the old mill house. "Excuse me, sir", I asked, "Who owns that piece of land?" "It's funny you should ask", said the builder, "Because there is something of a dispute about that. Some say an old lady in the village, some say the lock keeper, and some say a wealthy family in Goring."

We set out for the Cotswolds to research *Old Father's Source* and stayed at *The Thames Head Inn* (highly recommended). I had the idea of a geography teacher taking a ruler and drawing a line between Thames Head and Seven Springs and deciding the true source must be half way between. Before we got in the car, I took a map and a ruler and did just that. At the midway point we found the village of Duntisbourne Abbots. We drove there and spent about an hour behind the village, looking for a spring, and then we found one – right in the middle of the village, surrounded by a white picket fence. I began, myself, to think we'd found the true source. I asked a local if we might be right. "No sir, that ain't the Thames, that's the Dunt." But the topography appeared to give Ernest's theory some basis in fact.

Finally, we set out for Wallingford with my drama in mind concerning amateur theatricals and a fanatical dame-playing clergyman. Prior research revealed that Wallingford was the home of a long established amateur dramatic society – the *Sinodun Players*. When we arrived we stayed at the very hospitable *Coachmakers Arms Tavern (C.A.T.)*, which proved to be where the players met for their rehearsals. The night we were there turned out to be the 400th anniversary of Shakespeare's death, and we attended a marvellous production by the players at the Corn Exchange. We went along expecting amateurism, but the Shakespearean show, particularly Bottom the Weaver's play, was side-splittingly funny. To cap it all, a long serving former president of the players turned out to be a Dame – Dame Agatha Christie. There was a rather "lovey" thespian who constantly referred to *Midsummer Night's Dream* as "The Dream", and he later served, in my mind's eye, as the model for the Reverend Wright-Jesse.

If I ever publish a volume of the complete Monologues, I intend to produce a collection of maps and suggestions for "The Monologue Walks", so that my readers, if interested, can share in all the pleasure that Jenny and I have taken by the Thames researching these stories.

Acknowledgements

I would like to acknowledge my dear wife, Jenny, who clarified and incorporated the illustrations, formatted the text and designed the cover. Without Jenny's very talented assistance this book would not have been published. Jenny has endured twelve years of Monologue writing and learning with great patience and good humour, and she has served as my trusty prompter for all the tales in this volume. My thanks are due, also, to my helpful researcher, Mrs Shirley Egan; my former colleague, Mrs Ayesha Sodhi, who kindly typed the manuscript; and Miss Lizzie Willcocks who proof-read the typescript.

I would like to thank all those who have inspired, encouraged or listened to the Monologues over the years, in particular: Rodney and Pat Agambar, Paul and Angie Antrobus, Rev. Canon Peter Ball, Ralph Bell, Eric Brewer, David Bridel, Nick and Eleanor Butler, Andrew, Helen, Francis and Alice Carter, Daniel Carter, Joseph and George Carter, Sally Carter, Ian Curtis, Neil and Sue Davey, Christopher Dodd, Hilary Doran, Anders and Claire Eklund, Phil and Jackie Gray, Samuel Carter and Anna-Maria Hall, Steve and Catrina Hall, Andy and Louise Harper, Ken Harris, Nick and Medy Hart, Roy and Ann Hathaway, J. Milton-Hayes, Hannah and Martin Hefferland, Linda Henry, Pam Ireland, John "J.J." Jenkins P.A.C., Jerome K. Jerome, Dr. F.J. Laishley S.J., Pat Lake, Todd Longstaffe-Gowan, Derek Mason, Jadranka Michelotti (our friend in Venice),

Ian and Liz Mawson, Thanassis Mouikis, Tony and Angela O'Leary, "Pony-tail" Pete and Barbara Oakes, Dr. David Rands, Andrew "Stan" Stanley, Ali Stephens, Phil Sumner, Anthony Trollope, Fred Upstall, Jonny-Boy Wall and Hieromonk Theophan Willis ("Ken").

Finally, I would like to acknowledge my late friend and mentor in the "coarse" art of amateur theatricals, the Reverend Martin Hussey. Martin was the best pantomime dame I ever saw and in 1974 he supplied me with two pages of pantomime jokes. Among them was one joke that led me to conceive my first monologue, *The Tale of the Painted Sparrow*. This was it: "What is the difference between a lemon and a canary?" "I don't know." "Well, I won't be asking you to make me a gin and tonic." From this one joke, so much fun and nonsense has flowed, for me, and I hope for my audience too. So, thank you Martin.

By the same author

The Apollinarian Christologies: a study of the writings of Apollinarius of Laodicea, London, Hamley King Publishing 2011, ISBN 978-1-257-75976-7

The Weybridge Sailing Club Monologues London, Hamley King Publishing 2013, ISBN 978-1-291-62470-0